POEMS

قصـــائد

Al-Saddiq Al-Raddi

POEMS

الصادق الرضي

قصــائد

ENITHARMON PRESS

in association with

poetry
translation
centre

First published in 2008
by Enitharmon Press
26B Caversham Road
London NW5 2DU

www.enitharmon.co.uk

Distributed in the UK by
Central Books
99 Wallis Road
London E9 5LN

Distributed in the USA and Canada
by Dufour Editions Inc.
PO Box 7, Chester Springs
PA 19425, USA

Poems © Al-Saddiq Al-Raddi 2008
Translations from the Arabic © Sarah Maguire and Sabry Hafez
Introduction © Sabry Hafez

ISBN: 978-1-904634-77-5

Enitharmon Press gratefully acknowledges the financial support of
Arts Council England, London.

'Small Fox' has been published in *Poetry Review*.

British Library Cataloguing-in-Publication Data.
A catalogue record for this book is available
from the British Library.

Designed in Albertina by Libanus Press
and printed in England by
Cambridge University Press

Contents

Introduction	6
Small Fox	9
Garden Statues	11
In the Company of Michelangelo	15
Lamps	19
Everything	21
Only	23
Theatre	25

Introduction

Al-Saddiq Al-Raddi was born in Sudan in 1969 and grew up in Omdurman-Khartoum where he still lives. He started his career as a journalist and became the cultural editor of the Sudanese daily, *Al-Ayyam*, before moving to another newspaper, *Al-Sudani*, where he is currently the head of its cultural section. He is also the editor of the online website, *Sudanese Ink*. His poetic talents were revealed at an early age when in 1986, at the age of 17, he won the first prize in a major poetry competition; in the same year he became the youngest member elected to the Sudanese Writers' Union. In 1996, he published his first two collections, *Ghina' al-'Uzlah* (Songs of Solitude), and *Matahat al-Sultan* (The Sultan's Labyrinth) at once, revealing a body of work which immediately established him as both a distinguished new voice and as one of the formidable poets of his generation. His third collection, *Aqasi Shashat al-Isgha'* (The Limits of the Screen of Listening), appeared in 2000.

Al-Saddiq's advent onto the literary scene was part of a changing literary sensibility in Sudan in the 1990s. He belongs to a new generation of Sudanese writers whose cultural formation took place in the vacuum created by the exodus of most Sudanese intellectuals in the 1970s and 1980s who had been forced into exile as a result of increasingly harsh political and social pressures. As a result, his poetry is afflicted by a sense of orphanage, having little or no connection to the dominant tradition that prevailed in Sudan before these upheavals. This was later heightened, in Al-Saddiq's case, by his abandonment of traditional poetic metre with its lyricism and soothing musicality, when he chose to write what is known as 'prose poetry' in Arabic, which is analogous to free verse in English. The 1990s were the heyday of the prose poem in Arabic literature, which constituted a poetic rupture with the past; the new Sudanese poets, bewildered by the disastrous death of grand narratives, embraced its aesthetics of quiet contemplative reflections that were clearly suited to a world wallowing in defeat, crises and corruption.

Gone were the days of lyricism and hope, of collective vision and optimism, of oratory and joyous musicality, and the new poet was busy discovering the diction and form to suit his *Songs of Solitude*. He found guidance and solace in the poetry of the Sudanese, Muhammad Abdul-Hayy (1944–89), who died prematurely but is widely considered the father figure of Al-Saddiq's generation. Abdul-Hayy's poetry displayed a clear aversion to the hackneyed expressions and sonorous musicality that had dominated Sudanese poetry for generations. He shunned the predominance of ideological concerns, instead developing a keen interest in complex imagery, multilayered metaphors, mythic allusions, succinct diction, terse and well-structured poems, all the while keenly aware of the contradictions inherent in his position as an African poet writing in Arabic. These are also the types of poems that Al-Saddiq writes, for he once said that he attempts 'To radically change poetic language by enabling it to become multilayered, concerned as much with poetic structure as with thought, culture and metaphysics'. The metaphysical dimension of his poems is what distinguishes them from those of his contemporaries, and it is this multilayered structure that makes him so difficult to translate. Al-Saddiq also said, 'If the poem ceases to be multilayered, with a complex and sophisticated view of life, it ceases to be modern.'

The harsh climate and ruthless everyday reality of Sudan, with its cruel poverty and closed horizons, is balanced by and juxtaposed with its rich spirituality and fecund tradition of fantastic and mythical literature, which almost has a concrete presence in daily life. The poet captures these contradictions and renders them in poems like 'Lamps', 'Everything' and 'Theatre', poems which employ the binary of the beloved / homeland and transform it into an existential stance.

In 2005 he participated in the PTC's first World Poets' Tour, and this encounter with another culture sharpened his poetic desire for a new type of poetry which manifests itself in 'Small Fox', 'Garden Statues' and 'In the Company of Michelangelo' with their suppressed internal yearning. They open a new way forward in his poetry, and are a testimony of the valuable impact of the work of the PTC on the world of poetry. The 'drowning man' foundering 'in treacherous waters' of 'Everything' and the lamps that 'are extinguished / in the far-flung houses' of 'Lamps' are now being freshly cast in the bronze of that experience in 'Garden Statues'.

SABRY HAFEZ

ثعلب صغير

ثعلبٌ صغيرٌ
يمرحُ في قلبكِ الملوَّثْ
أفلحَ في الهطول **تلك الليلة**
وجهُكِ
غمرَه بالصعلكةِ واليُتم..
بما يكفي ويفيضْ..

تلك الليلة أوحشتْ ممرَّكِ الأثيرَ نحوي
أوحشتكِ كثيراً
أوحشتْ قمراً يتعلَّمُ الأسماءْ
فلم نعد بحاجةٍ لإناءٍ يتكسَّرُ
إثرَ رقصةِ السنجابْ
وتعلُّقِ الظُلمة بآخرِ قطراتِ النبيذْ

عنِّي: مَللتُ بالظمأُ
يدي أرْعشتها رغبةُ الحنوِّ
وما من ثعلبٍ آخرَ في الطريقْ!

الخرطوم 14 يونيو 2006

SMALL FOX

Suddenly – a small fox, playful,
floods your wounded heart with joy
He searches your face with his singular gaze,
knows you're at one with his vagabond stance

That very night I longed for you,
I missed your exquisite arousal,
I yearned for that moon we named together
After the squirrel had slipped off,
we needed nothing
but night, and the last dregs of wine

And as for me – I am drunk with thirst,
I am shaking with desire for you –
but here there's not a fox to be found

Khartoum, 14 June 2006

تماثيل الحدائق

الليلة الأخيرة ...
الليلة الأولى ...
... بينهما البحيرة الصافيةْ
....
تركتَ كأسَ الذكرى للذكرى
تنظم ذراته ذهب الليلات - جميعاً
تركتَ صوته — علي فاركا توري
يسبحُ
في فضّةِ الغرفة
المفروشة بلآلئ الساعات و الدقائقْ
تركتَ أصابعَ تائهةٍ في إلفة (كيبورد) راحلْ
الحصانَ الخشبيَّ الصغيرْ
الدبَّ القطنَ على الكرسيِّ
الحدائقَ في الجوار
الشمسَ تمرحُ في الثامنةِ مساءً
تركتَ نافذةً مشرعةً
صباحاً يلبسُ زيَّ صباحْ
تركتَ الزهرةَ تكدحُ كدحاً
فتلاقيه ..
تركته — عمداً :
الطاؤس يعملُ — مأسوراً — في حقل الجمالْ
... ...
لم يَعُدْ - ما تبقّى من الوقتِ ..
.. من ليلته تلك..

GARDEN STATUES

The last night . . .
the first night . . .
 . . . between them – clarity
. . . .

You left that glass of memory to memory –
    let its essence transmute all these nights into gold

You left the voice of Ali Farka Toure
    soaring
    through the silvered light of a room,
    a room inlaid with the jewels of minutes and hours

You left your hands lost in the familiar characters of a vanishing keyboard

You left a wooden rocking-horse
    an old teddy-bear propped on a chair
    the neighbouring gardens

You left the sun still toying with the sky at eight in the evening

You left a window open
    on a morning arrayed with morning

You left a flower labouring towards morning

You deliberately left that peacock arrested in the field of beauty

. . . .

Whatever time is left of that night
    will never return . . .
These jewels will never return
A sail will never quench its thirst for the horizon

لم تَعُدْ اليواقيتُ ..
لم يَعُدْ الظمأُ من ألقِ الشراعْ

بينما..
عدتَ من (برونز) التجربةْ
مُلتهماً — كاملاً

عدتَ من صدفٍ
من فخارٍ - بلا زخرف
عادتْ الأيامُ — بلا هدايا
عادتْ وصاياكَ
عادَ السكونْ !

5 أبريل 2006م لندن

And when you left
> you were cast in the bronze of that experience
> you were consumed and yet complete
> you were fashioned from mother-of-pearl
> you were made of unadorned clay

Weekdays returned, empty handed
Routine returned

And silence reigned

London, 5 April 2006

صحبة مايكل انجلو

1

الملوكُ الذين مضوا ..
تركوا أثراً اسمه نسيانَهم
مثل (أليس) أو (كوش) ..إلخ .

تركوا: تيجاناً ممعنةً في غرابةٍ
بقايا هياكلَ عظميةٍ
رؤوسَ أسماكَ — أسماءَ يصعبُ نُطْقَها
مراودَ كُحلٍ — وصايا — مدائحَ منقوشةً على حجرْ

بيدَ أنِّي تركتُكِ
أنتِ المُضاءَةُ بي
أينما حملتَكِ عروشُكِ
دماً طازجاً في شرايينَ تَفنَى
و يصعبُ نسيانُكِ !

2

عند روما القديمة — أبواب روما القديمة
تصحبُني ممعناً في صرامة الدقّة المتناهيةْ
لتصوركَ الخيطَ في ثقبه الأرهفَ
لتصوركَ الخطَّ والمنحنى
تصحبُني في صداقةِ الحجرْ
يدٌ ليدٍ

IN THE COMPANY OF MICHELANGELO

    1

The kings who have gone
left us the relics of their forgettable names –
like Aleece or Kush

They left us their peculiar crowns
shards of skeletons
fish-heads
unpronounceable words
kohl-sticks
commandments
and eulogies graven in stone

Yet you are
       lit up beside me
       wherever your throne sets down
Live blood in dead veins –
you truly are unforgettable

    2

You accompany me
to the gates of ancient Rome
reaching the ends of perfection
as you envisage grace threading each tender aperture
as you envisage the faultless line and the perfect circle

Let us be brothers in stone
hand in hand
fingers entwined –
and then,

أصابعُ لأصابعَ
ثم ..
في مدخلِ الحانةِ
نقرعُ كأساً بكأسٍ
تضعُ النقطةَ التاليةُ
في صفحةِ وجهٍ يتفرَّسُ تاريخَه

3

أينا المفتاحُ – عند بابكَ أو عند بابي ؟!

4

يَسْعَدُ الصمتُ
يَسْعَدُ الحال
يسعد نُطْقُ الصورْ
كلما تُركَ المقعد خاليا
كلما توارى صاحب المعطف
كلما سُمعت شهقةُ العتمة الخفيفة
العناق — ميثولوجيا الحضور!

5

ما الحكمة ..؟!

30 مارس 2006م– لندن

on the threshold of a bar
we clink our glasses
as you add the last touch
to a face already dreaming its history

    3

Which of us is the key?
Your door or mine?

    4

Silence is bliss
Life is bliss
Creation is bliss

          Even though his chair is empty
          even though he is gone
          darkness is alight
with the presence of his embrace

    5

What is the key?

London, 30 March 2006

مصابيح

في الماءِ
في صَمْتي وقُرْبِكِ
في نارٍ - وَحْدَهَا تَجمَعُنا
أَطْفُو ..
ووحْدَكِ قد تُنادِينَ عَلَيَّ!

....

يدخُلُ الطائرُ طقسَ الأخضرِ
مثلَ الوَتَر
بَرْقٌ يَرفُّ على العين كالسِّرِّ
تنحني قُبْلَةٌ في القوسْ
يَسْتَمِرُّ المطر!

في الشوارعِ لم يَعُدْ أصدقائي
في البيوتِ البعيدةِ عن بعضِها
لم تَعُدِ المصابيحْ
في القلب عادتْ رَجَّةُ النَّبْضِ المبعثرْ
لكنَّكِ تَرْمينَ المناديلَ على الرَّاحلِ
والباقي على نورِ الصباح!

LAMPS

In the water
in silence at your side
in a fire that draws us close
I drift –
and only you can call me

. . . .
A bird enters spring
like a lance
Your eyes flash their secrets
A kiss grazes the rainbow
The rain rains

But the streets are empty of my friends
Lamps are extinguished
in the far-flung houses
and the lost heart echoes in its lonely chamber

You give your blessings to those who depart
and leave the rest to fate

كلُّ شَيْءْ

إطلق الرِّيحَ من فَمِ الصيّادِ
إلى هيكلِ المُرْكَبِ ، من عُمْقِ الشراعِ
وفَكِّكْ الرُّبُطِ عن فمِ النهرِ
أُصرخْ
أيها الغريقُ
في اللُّجَجِ الدائرةْ

يبدأُ النهرُ من عاداته، ساكناً
يبدأُ الشاطئُ لَمِّ الشموسِ
من أفواهِ السمكِ المَيِّتِ
يبدأُ طَهْوِ الظلال
من الرائحةِ، كنسَ الحصى

لكنَّ الهدوء — الريح — أصوات
الذين يركبون المقالع — لكنَّ السكونْ

يبحرونَ من ليلٍ بعيدٍ
يحفرونَ الماءَ بالصبر العتيدِ
وينظرونَ العَتْمَةَ

بينما أبحرتَ قُربَ الصباحِ
من محاياتٍ التي في صدرهَا
أُثبتَّ مَعْنى
قادماً منها وتطلبُ الضفةَ — حضرةَ العمرِ وأوراقِ الهويةِ
بينما أخرى تؤجِّركَ البسيطةَ
بين عينيها
وتطلبُ صفوَ أوراقِ الكتابةِ – كلُّ شَيْءْ !

EVERYTHING

Let the wind blow from a fisherman's mouth,
from the span of a sail to the shell of a boat,
unlocking the mouth of the river –
So, shout, drowning man, when you founder
in treacherous waters

At dawn, the river embarks in silence
Riverbanks glean suns from the scales of dead fish
Jostled by eddies, the aroma of flotsam and jetsam
bakes in the shade

Becalmed, a breeze freights the stillness
Sails lazily unfurl

They sail all night from afar,
ploughing the river with ritual persistence,
staring darkness straight in the eye

You set sail at dawn,
infused with the tincture of a heart
that had beached your whole life ashore

And yet, another beloved
is offering you heaven on earth in her glance,
demanding only the perfection of poetry – everything!

فقط

ظهيرةٌ كسولَةٌ
تقودني من طيوفكِ إلى كوب الشاي
إلى عناق الحيرةِ
وفقَ مزاجٍ صاخبٍ بالفضولِ
أتحسَّسُ قاعَ الرائحةِ
التي تبقى
من حضورِكِ
أحدسُ لوناً يُضيئُكِ من الظلِّ
وبقايا الأقاصيصِ عنكِ
يا خاطئةْ
كالرسولة من دهنِ الأحاديث تنسلِّينَ
من فواكه الرائحة الناعسةْ
وتسيِّجينَ الخواطرَ بأصنافِ البداهاتْ

ONLY

A lazy noon
stirs me from your memory to this glass of tea
and a wondering embrace

In a mood busy with inquisitiveness
I smell the lees of the scent
that lingers
behind you

I sense your shade in the shadows
in the dregs of all that gossip –
Oh you sinner!

Like a rumoured prophet's advent
you slide from the ripe fruit of sleep
afire with ideas, your flashing wit

مسرح

1

كلُّ هذه الحروبْ
ليصبحَ العَالمُ مُوحِشاً
من أجل أن يصدأ البيتُ
كي تنامَ
موجَّعاً بالكارثةْ
كلُّ هذا الحبّ
من أجل أن تنطقَ العظامُ بــ لا أحدْ
كلُّ هذا الموتْ
لأجل أن نلتقي
فقطْ ؟!

2

أُكتبْ
فَلْيَشْتَعِلَ العالمُ فيك
من بين يديكَ
ولْتَشْتَعِلْ بالبذاءةِ روحُ الجسدْ
فيكَ ما يَمْحُو ويُمْحَى
داءُ الحِبْرْ
عَرَقُ الشُّغْلِ واللّهاثِ
من بيتٍ وصالةٍ
لشارعٍ وعراءْ
أُكتبْ
بمشيئةِ العارفِ

THEATRE

1

All these wars
make the world unhomely
make homes rust apart
make you fall asleep, riddled with calamities

All this love
yet loneliness still cuts you to the bone

All this death
just so we can meet –
nothing more?

2

Write
to set the world ablaze
so poetry quickens in your hands
and inflames you with desire

Write, and wipe the slate
Infected by writing
you sweat in agony
from a bedsit
to the street and out into the wild

Write
in full knowledge

بكلِّ ما بين يديك
من قصبٍ وخيوطْ
بخبرة الرائي، ما يحرِّكُ الجسدَ
يفيدُ الفضاءْ

3

هذا العالمُ الصغيرُ — أمامَكَ
المصنوعُ من القشِّ والدُّبَارَةِ والمَلَلْ
الذي يتسرَّبُ من بين الأصابعِ كالأحلامِ
تَذْرُوه الروحُ
وتمتصُّه — أنتَ — كالرائحةْ

هل تخافُ الحشراتِ — تحتمي فيه من النور كلَّه
أم تخافُ الدَمَ — تَعَافُ براءةَ السيِّدِ فيه
تختشي من الأصابعِ والخفَّةِ والشموعْ ؟!

هذا العالَمُ المفتوحُ أمامك
يُغنيكَ عن السؤال
هل يُساوي ثمنَ الحبرِ الذي كُتِبَ به
ثمنُ الدمعِ — بَعدُ — لم يَحَفّْ؟!

4

معقوفٌ — زمنُ النورِ — تحسَّه يلسعُ صفحةَ الوجهِ
تحسَّه هي
وهي تمسحُ — الخوانَ — حائلَ اللَّونِ

of everything that's in your hands
both quill and string at your disposal
Write
certain of what electrifies the body
sure of how to rig the scene

    3

This little world beneath you
made of boredom, balsawood and string
jerks between your fingers in a dream
Spirited away
you drink it in like scent

Are you scared of scorpions? Are you scared of blood?
Take refuge in the wings
But beware the spotlights, beware of being fingered

This little world beneath you
is here to give you all the answers
Is it worth the precious ink that wrote it –
the cost of these fresh tears?

    4

Light stings the page of your face
And it strikes her
as she dusts the faded wardrobe near the bed –
like a dagger, suddenly

خلفَ السرير
لكنه بغتةً كالخنجرِ
يدخلُ قلبَ الظُلمَةِ
يُبْحِرُ ببهاءِ العالمِ كلّهِ
بطينِ العناقِ وعتمةِ التعرّفِ بالبَلَلْ
يتركُ الوجَه مُرتبكاً
يتركُهَا بِاضْطِجَاعَةِ الذهولْ !

5

واحدٌ، الأبيضُ
واحدةٌ، الجهاتْ
كلُّنا نتشبَّثُ بالحيرةِ والحبرِ والرحيلْ

نَسكنُ أحلامَنا وننشرُ المناديلَ
نُبشِّرُ الحاناتِ بالمرايا والغثيانْ
بدوائرِ الدخانِ والحكايا
من كلِّ أبيضَ نعدِّدُ الحبرَ
يتحدُ الدمعُ
تنبثقُ الدهشةُ
من كلِّ جهةٍ تسطعُ القبورْ !

6

أراكَ مُنتظراً باباً وراءَكَ
يُفْتَحُ بالرَّبَابَةِ
كي تَدْخُلَ الماضي بمستقبلٍ لا يُشِينْ

it rends the dark
blazing with the whole world's brilliance,
leaves her flushed,
spoored, wet
and flat out in astonishment

    5

We latch on to bewilderment, to ink, and to departure
Living in our dreams, unfurling handkerchiefs,
we bring news to the bars of mirrors and nausea,
smoke-rings, gossip, tales
From the oneness of white we plumb our ink,
from the oneness of all directions
Tears merge
Surprise arrives
All around you tombstones rise

    6

Waiting in front of a door that's behind you,
I watch it open with a rabab
so you can go back to the past with your spotless future,
refilling your boats with light after they'd rotted through ashore,
restocking the wares of your mighty stories
like a bird refurbishing its nest

مضيئاً قواربكَ التي تحطَّمَتْ من الرُّسُوِّ
مُقْعِداً أقاصيكَ الرحيبة
مثلَ دَانٍ
طائراً تمتحنُ السجيّة

والذين من أمامكَ في السَّهْوْ
يَعْتَمِرونَ، تمرُّ فوانيسُهم عبرَ بابكَ
مُسْوَدَّةً صحائفُ الفجرِ
من أثرِ الغروبْ

كانَ وَجهُكَ يُعْرَفُ
والبابُ خلفَكَ
وجَهُ الذي من أمامكَ
كيفَ ؟!

.... تدخلُ الماضي بمستقبلٍ لا يشينْ !

7

هذا ثمنُ الحربِ: ولاؤكَ الدائمُ
لكفاءَةِ التهريجِ
تِكْنيكِ البراءَةْ
هذا ثمنُ الحبِّ: عقوقُكَ الدائمُ لأُبُوَّةِ التِّكْنِيكِ
أُمُومَةِ الكفاءَةْ

هذا ثمنُ الموتِ: بقاؤكَ الدائمُ حيّاً
بقبرِ الحبِّ وساحةِ الحربِ
بقاؤكَ الدائمُ في هُوَّةِ الطَّاعةِ
في مَسْقَطِ العالمْ !.

Those who went before you
live in a stupor,
their lanterns barging through your door
The flush of dawn
blackened
by the taint of dusk
Your face is familiar,
but what about the face in front of you
faced towards the door behind you?
. . . . as you go back to the past with your blameless future

    7

The price of war: perpetual loyalty;
eschewing tomfoolery;
feigning naivety

The price of love: ceaseless quarrels
with the fathers of procedures
and the mothers of proficiency

The price of death: eternal life
in the grave of love and the theatre of war
Life at the ends of obedience
Life at the end of the world